Alfons J. Dietz and D

LONG REINING

The Correct Approach

CONTENTS

Imprint

Copyright of original edition ©2002
Cadmos Verlag GmbH, Lüneberg.
Copyright of this edition ©2003 Cadmos Verlag.
Translation: Konstanze Allsopp
Layout: Ravenstein
Front cover and inside photos : Daniela Bolze
Drawings: Christina Krumm
Print: Westermann Druck, Zwickau

All rights are reserved.
Reprint or storage in electronic media only with
written permission from the publisher.
Printed in Germany.
ISBN 3-86127-936-3

Long reins enables the trainer to place his horse between the aids.

vity for the movements of the horse, can use this training to supple their horses very effectively and thus prepare it for being ridden. This is because the opportunities to recognise, to control in a focused manner, and to manipulate the movements of the horse are far greater from the ground. This is of particular advantage when training young horses. And of course, it is also much easier for the horse to perform the required tasks, if it does not have to carry around the unbalanced weight of a rider.

Unlike working with a normal lunge rein, with long reins the trainer has the opportunity to "place the horse between the rider's aids" with the aid of the second rein, in order to give aids on the offside as well as the nearside. The outside lunge rein not only keeps the horse on the bit but can also, to a certain extent, take over the role of the outside leg. Depending on the type of attachment chosen, all exercises on the ground as well as movements above the ground can be performed, even jumping fences.

Apart from forming the basic groundwork for the classical art of equitation, working with the long reins also benefits those, who want to:
• train young horses
• improve the rhythm, impulsion and thrust
  of the horse
• release physical and psychological blockages
• exercise the horse efficiently in a short session
• apply corrective measures.

Why Work With Long Reins?

Few methods for training horses are as underestimated as work with long reins. For horses which perform the classic art of movements above the ground, it is an essential part of the training programme, but few people appreciate how practical this training is, especially for non-professional riders and the like, and how much it helps their horses. In particular, less experienced riders who are not yet fluent in movements on horseback and who lack the high degree of sensiti-

The Equipment

The equipment needed for working with the lunge and long reins can range from cheap but effective, to expensive and top of the range. Anyone who wants to ensure that he does everything completely right will first and foremost need a well-fitting lunge cavesson with three rings, especially when working with a young horse. This ensures that the horse's mouth is treated with care. However, if you do not wish to invest in this piece of equipment, you can work with a normal snaffle bridle. In this case it is important, particularly in the beginning, to make sure the lungeing ring is fenced in, so that the horse does not have to be kept on the circle with the aids of the reins, but to begin with will instead remain on the bit through contact with the outside rein and with the help of the school boundary. The lunge rein itself should definitely be of good quality. It should consist of an approximately 14 metres long cotton rein. The rein should be neither too thick, as this

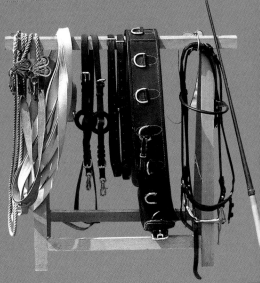

Working with the long reins: double lunge rein with deflection rollers, side reins, lungeing roller with D-rings, full cheek snaffle bit, lungeing whip.

would mean having too much in one's hands, nor too thin, so that the rein is not too hard in the trainer's hands. The ends are fitted with two thin round pieces of rope with a spring clip each, which can be hooked into the snaffle rings. The pieces of rope ensure that the reins run more smoothly through the lungeing roller rings. This is imperative because otherwise the influence on the horse's mouth would be far too severe. The use of deflection rollers is also recommended, to further make the contact as light as possible. You will find deflection rollers in certain very well-equipped equestrian shops, but possibly more readily in ship's chandlers selling sailing equipment. They allow the trainer to use the reins with a particularly sensitive touch. And the more sensitively the horse is handled, the more sensitively it will react.

It is of great importance that the lungeing roller fits correctly. It should be equipped with at least four fixed rings which should be set not too

Working with the lunge: soft cotton lunge rein, a number of side reins, lungeing roller with several D-rings, lunge cavesson and full cheek snaffle bit, lungeing whip.

high on the lungeing roller. Use a well-padded numnah or a piece of sheepskin to ensure that the lungeing roller does not chafe the horse's withers. Good lungeing rollers are already padded to correctly fit the horse's anatomy.

For basic training, it is sufficient to have a light lungeing whip, which should have a lash which is long enough to be able to touch the horse with it on the respective points under all circumstances.

Note

Make sure that the whip is light in the hand. Otherwise it will become a serious handicap after a few minutes and the application of light aids will not be possible.

Young and headstrong horses should initially be lunged with a well-fitting lunge cavesson with an underlying full cheek snaffle bit, in order to treat their mouths with care.

Another important thing: gloves. Never lunge your horse without wearing gloves. You will lose your ability to control the horse should it get startled, take off, or simply refuse to co-operate. What you will be left with is burn marks on the palms of your hands which will be painful for a number of days.

For most horses, in particular youngsters, it is recommended that they should perform their first lungeing and long rein sessions in a well-fenced area. A small square area or a lungeing circle which should have a diameter of approximately 20 metres, depending on the size of the horse, will do well. The presence of a visual outer restriction and contact allows the horse to concentrate better on the trainer's aids. And please make sure to wear sturdy boots or shoes, so that you don't lose your balance should you ever need to use your entire weight to control the horse. These rules apply to all work with horses.

To begin with the horse needs to be able to warm up and loosen its muscles without being hampered with side reins.

Only side reins have any gymnastic effect on the horse, if the trainer works with a simple lunge rein.

What the Horse Needs to Know

Filled with enthusiasm having read this book, before starting to lunge your horse, both man and animal need to fulfil a certain number of pre-requisites. The horse can only be trained on the long reins after it has learned all commands during normal single lungeing lessons which its trainer asks for from the centre. As ever, a good preparation for working on the lunge is the so-called "join-up" or free lungeing in a round pen. In this book on working with the long reins, I assume that the horse has learned to work freely in the round pen as well as the normal lungeing work.

Note

Make sure that the round pen is really secure with a high fence. Some horses avoid having to work by trying to force their way through or over the fence.

If you do not have a fixed round pen available, start working the horse on the lunge from the start.

The horse's head must never be forced behind the vertical line with the side reins.

What the Trainer Needs to Know

In order to work safely and productively with horses, you need to have a thorough knowledge of the horse's behaviour patterns. Also, you must know how to handle all the artificial aids which are used when working with the horse. In other words, you need to be able to control the equipment before using it on the horse.

Positioning and Handling of the Whip

The principal factors in the communication between trainer and horse are the position of the trainer holding the lunge and the position of the whip. The more you show the horse your front profile with your shoulders, the more dominant and thereby forwards driving your effect on the horse will be. The same goes for the positioning of the body relative to the horse: the more you "move behind the horse", the faster it will go. The more you move to its shoulder, the slower the horse gets. In front of the head line of the horse, the trainer acts as a brake. In order not to always have to keep changing your own position, this task is taken over by the whip. It acts as an elongation of the trainer's arm.

In addition to the general position of the whip, the method of application and the point at which it touches the horse also have an effect. To drive the horse forwards, it is usually sufficient to place the lash of the whip behind the back hoof of the horse with a light flick. If that should not suffice, touch the horse lightly at the level of the hock. The whip lash should always be swung in an upward motion to ask the horse to increase its pace. Downward movement of the whip should be reserved exclusively for punishment (although this should be avoided, as the whip is not intended principally as an instrument of punishment).

To stop the horse from turning in towards you, point the whip at its shoulder. If that does not work, swing the whip in an upward motion against the horse's shoulder. (N.B. Never hit the horse on the head.) To slow the horse down, pass the whip above or under the lunge rein and point towards the horse's head. This needs to be done with care, as some horses are whip-shy and ,ay react in the wrong way. Very often, just showing the handle of the whip is enough. If the horse does not react, swing the whip

Note

Practise the handling of the lunge whip on aluminium cans, rather than with the horse itself. The lash of the whip should ideally be made from leather and be sufficiently pliable. Swing the whip in a supple movement from the wrist so that the whip lash swings forwards. Only after you have mastered hitting the empty cans spot on, should you attempt to use the whip on the horse.

lash in an upward movement in front of the head. If this does not have the desired effect either, turn your shoulder distinctly towards the front of the horse's head.

For the walk, the whip lash is pointed at the height of the hind fetlock joint ...

... for the trot at the level of the hock ...

... and for the canter at the level of the hip joint.

To ask the horse to halt, the whip is placed in front of the horse's head.

The lunge rein needs to be held and handled in an orderly manner ...

... and under no circumstances get into such a disorderly muddle of loops.

Voice Commands

Always combine your body language with voice commands. It matters little what terms you use, as long as you stick to them. However, using the commonly known commands will allow anybody else to lunge your horse without the danger of misunderstandings. A low and calm, drawn-out "Whoa" should prove effective in slowing the horse down, whereas the trainer should raise his voice and give the commands "And walk on", "And trot on", or "And canter on", spoken with a crisp voice, when the horse is asked to increase its pace.

This use of verbal commands acts in the same way as half-halts, preparing the horse for the following action. To ask the horse to halt, the terms "Halt" or "Stand" are used. You will be able to drive the horse forwards faster, or slow it down, with the different intonation of your voice alone, depending on how loudly, quietly, calmly or aggressively you talk.

But avoid talking to your horse non-stop, as this will soon bore it and it will cease to listen.

It is very important however to praise your horse with your voice immediately at the right moment. The best words are "Good boy [girl]". Horses learn through praise, not punishment.

To take up the lunge rein when moving towards the horse ...

... walk step by step, making large loops that do not touch the ground ...

Handling the Lunge Rein

In addition to the correct use of the lunge whip, the trainer also has to become used to handling the lunge rein – at first, without the horse. With the help of an assistant, practise how to roll up the rein, letting the loops run through your hands and also taking them up again. Always make sure that you don't wrap any loops around your hand. Loops around the hand can be very dangerous and have squashed many a trainer's hand, in extreme cases even tearing them off.

... ensuring that you remain securely in control at all times.

Always take up the loops in such a way that you place them into your left hand with the right, if the horse is on the left rein. On the right rein, the loops are placed into the right hand with the left. This way you can always let out the lunge rein without ending up with a mess of twisted rein or having the loops being pulled tighter and tighter. Make sure when looping the lunge rein that the loops are not too large, otherwise you could step into them, or too small, which means you end up holding too much rein in your hand. If you handle the reins with one hand, the index finger should always separate both reins.

Initially, you should hold the reins with both hands. As you and the horse become more experienced, you can change to single-handed control of the lunge reins, which means a more sensitive application of the aids. Handling the lunge reins with one hand also allows you to give more refined driving aids with the lunge whip, and you can engage the horse's hindquarters to a greater extent.

Note

A small leather strap can be used to attach the double lunge rein to the lungeing roller, making it easier to lead the horse before and after lungeing.

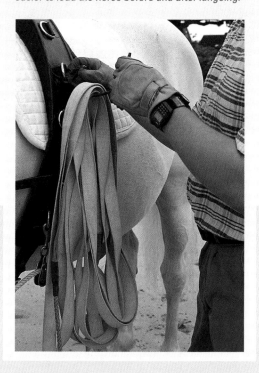

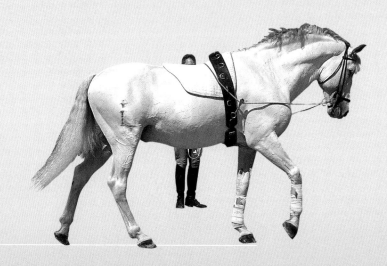

If possible, the trainer should use an experienced assistant for his first attempts at working the horse on the lunge and long reins.

The First Time

You should not have any problems working your horse on the long reins for the first time if it has already been thoroughly trained on the single lunge rein.

For the sake of safety, however, you should arrange to have at hand someone to help who will stand next to the horse's head until everything has been fastened and fitted properly. The assistant leads the horse to its place and walks beside it until you have arranged the loops of the lunge rein and positioned the whip correctly. Nevertheless, it is possible to tackle this first hurdle without assistance, together with your horse.

Anybody who is able to lunge his horse with sufficiently long side reins (do not force the horse's head behind the vertical!), can also make the work with the long reins easier by initially keeping the side reins fitted.

When first working with the long reins, you should fit the horse with a lunge cavesson, rather than taking up contact with the horse's mouth via the snaffle bit.

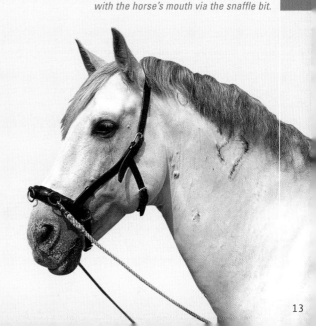

13

If the reins have been attached in the V-formation the trainer has a softer influence with the inside lunge rein ...

... while the outside lunge rein gently gives the horse a framework.

V-Attachment

Any work with long reins start with the so-called "V-attachment". With this type of attachment the reins are attached differently on the inside and outside of the horse. The outside rein is placed over the back of the horse, passed through one of the middle rings of the lungeing roller and is fitted directly to the ring of the snaffle bit. The inside rein, on the other hand, is first passed through the ring of the snaffle bit from the front and then attached to the lungeing roller with its spring clip. It is best to pass the outside rein through a lower ring than that to which the inside rein is attached, but only as long as the trainer works with the V-attachment. It is not possible to carry out smooth changes of the reins with the V-attachment, as the horse needs to be fitted differently for each change of rein.

It is a matter of the natural head carriage of the horse and its level of training, to decide which rol-ler rings to use. The head should not be pulled against the shoulder, and the horse should not be forced into position. On the other hand, the effect of the lunge reins should not simply vanish into thin air.

The advantage of the V-attachment is that it provides a more refined application of the aids for the horse. The trainer has far more sophisticated opportunities to loosen the horse from the inside out by slightly relaxing the inside rein. The variable application of the aids is the bonus of working with long reins.

The outside rein, attached slightly lower, not only provides a framework for the horse but also keeps it on the circle track if the horse tries to push in towards the centre. In addition, the handle of the whip is used pointing to the head or the shoulder of the horse to stop it from veering inwards. The inside lunge rein ensures that the horse does not pull to the outside if the lungeing area is not fenced off as a circle. Attaching the inside lunge rein higher up ensures that the horse's head is not pulled in towards its chest in the manner of draw reins, in the event of too severely handling the inside lunge rein.

When the horse is lunged with long reins, it should always keep light contact with the reins. However, instead of a clumsy shortening of the reins, the horse is encouraged to go on the bit by gentle driving aids with the whip. In this way, it is driven onto the bit through engagement of the hindquarters. In fact, the horse is encouraged to come on the bit in the same way as it would be when being ridden correctly.

To begin with, simply let the horse walk around you on a circle. Try to encourage it to move forwards when using the whip, keeping it evenly between the two reins and framed in loosely from behind. If you are fairly secure and have found your own second inner circle, you can slowly begin working on transitions. Please ensure that you do not stand rooted on one spot in the centre of the circle, but follow the horse on a smaller inner circle of your own. This way you will acquire a better feeling for the horse and also present it with a more distinct body language than if you only turn around on your heel in the centre.

Young horses in particular should be lunged with very loose reins to begin with, in order not to frighten them.

Note

When using half-halts always remember that they are applied one-to-one in the horse's mouth. If you pull back your right arm by 30 centimetres to apply a half-halt to the outside rein, precisely these 30 centimetres will act at the corner of the horse's mouth. Transformed into ridden work, this would represent a fearsome half-halt – and it will be the same on the long reins. Therefore please remember: use light aids!

The first steps

The trainer has two options to begin working with long reins. The first is that he attaches the lunge reins on the track and then moves backwards a few steps to find his own position. Only then does he ask the horse to move forward. Many trainers work this way. The risk here is that the horse will simply follow the trainer. In horse language terms, however, it signals a victory for the horse as the trainer is moving back (retreating), whereas the horse stands firm in position.

The alternative, and better, option is that you attach the lunge reins in the centre of the circle. Once you are ready, take up the reins loosely and send the horse out onto the track of the lunge circle with the command "Move out" (it will need to have learnt this command, however), with the whip stock pointing to the horse's shoulder.

Whichever approach you adopt, it is very important that the animal does not start moving until you have given the clear voice command, supported by the lungeing whip.

A variation of the second option involves working with an assistant, who leads the horse out to the circle track while you are giving it the correct signals described above from your position in the centre.

Once everybody is in place, you have to make sure that the horse moves off at an energetic four-beat walk, without hurrying or dragging its feet. If the horse slows down you must ask it repeatedly to move faster by using the voice command "And walk/ trot/canter on", immediately supporting this command by placing the lash of the whip just behind the horse. If the horse moves at the pace you want it to, there is no need to swing the whip about, as many people do. The whip is an aid, just like the half-halt, and should only be applied when it is really needed.

If on the other hand, the horse moves too fast, initially calm it down with your voice ("Whoa, steady on, calm down"). Then shorten the lunge reins slightly, always letting them out again so that the horse cannot simply rest its weight on the bit, and slowly move the whip forward underneath the lunge rein, until the moment is right to use it in a calming manner. The horse should know this from previous lungeing.

Long reins also give you the opportunity to slow the horse down towards the fencing by using distinct half-halts on the outside rein, bending the horse's head and neck to the outside. This however should only be used as a last resort and is not an elegant solution to the problem. If you bend the horse to the outside, it is important to give with the inner rein.

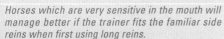

Horses which are very sensitive in the mouth will manage better if the trainer fits the familiar side reins when first using long reins.

To begin with, in particular, it may be necessery to bring the horse to a halt with a distinct outward bend in the direction of the fence.

The Halt

Basically the aids are the same as those for slowing down. First warn your horse with the voice ("Whoa", "Halt" or "Stand"). You yourself stop in one place and don't follow the horse anymore. Basically, let the horse move into the lunge reins, so to speak. If it does not react to this, give distinct half-halts with the outside rein and bring it to a halt in the direction of the fence. Pass the whip to the front of the horse and lift it up so that the horse also has a visual boundary from the front. Praise it lavishly when it comes to a halt. Don't wait too long before asking the horse to move forwards again, as it could otherwise move on of its own accord or come towards you in the centre. Instead ask it to move forward again at the walk after a few seconds.

This photograph demonstrates very nicely how the horse is in the framework of the lunge reins and whip aids

Note

Avoid practising to halt on a day on which the horse is on its toes already, but rather at the end of a calm, relaxed phase at the walk. Always remember to remain patient, if things don't work out as planned immediately.

Using the V-attachment the horse should learn the following:
• to move calmly between the two lunge reins
• to learn to change the tempo (the number of strides per minute) in all three basic paces
• to search for and come on the bit
• the change between bending and straightening its body
• the fact that the lunge rein passes over its flanks

On the Bit

As soon as the horse has become accustomed to the two lunge, you can start encouraging it to look for contact with the bit by applying gentle half-halts while driving the horse forward carefully with the whip. As the lunge reins are not fixed in position (unlike the immobile side reins), you can let the horse stretch its head down to the ground in its search for the bit. This is a marvellous stretching exercise which causes the entire top line of the horse to arch itself upwards. Initially, one of the most important aims of working with long reins is this repeated stretching of the horse. Once it always works at the walk, you can also try this exercise at the trot and canter. If the horse still walks around with its head held high and its back hollowed out after two or three rounds on the circle, you will have to reduce the tempo again. You

Here the horse, overtracking well, is kept on the bit with both reins in one hand, ...

... so that it stretches its nose to the ground with an arched back, once the reins have been slackened.

will be able to take the horse out of the low stretched posture again by shortening the reins slightly and at the same time drive it forwards with increased force from behind with the whip. If the aids are applied correctly, the horse will shorten itself from the rear to the front of its own accord and will collect itself slightly by engaging its back legs to step further under the centre of gravity (the place where the rider's weight will be centred on the horse's back). Please ensure that you always drive the horse from behind, as it will only pull its nose in otherwise, with the hindquarters trailing

– not something to aim for either on the lunge or under the rider.

Note

Always remember that your own body language also acts as an aid for the horse. The more relaxed and at ease your own movements, the more this will transmit itself to the horse. This is of particular importance for rhythmic, collected lungeing. The more upright, full of energy, and collected you are, the easier it becomes for the horse.

The Walk

At the walk the horse should learn to walk forwards energetically without dragging its feet. Make sure that the horse engages its hindquarters and overtracks well. You can achieve this by using the driving aids with more vigour. The walk is the pace at which all new exercises are practised first and where the horse first stretches and relaxes forwards and downward. In most cases horses calm down more easily at the walk. With extremely lively horses however it may be more sensible to work them at the trot first in order to burn off any excess energy. However, there is no real gymnastic effect during this phase.

The walk should be full of impulsion but not hurried.
Here the horse is lunged in the direct attachment.

The trot is ideal for working on
the impulsion of the horse.

The Trot

The trot is the best phase for the horse to develop impulsion. However it is equally important to make sure that the hindquarters are engaged and the horse overtracks sufficiently, without rushing forwards. If the horse is able to stretch forwards and downward at the trot, the trainer can try to ask for a rhythmic and slightly collected pace. Remember to keep your hands light; only take up the lunge reins with increased hold for a short period, then relax them again as soon as possible. The trainer must prevent the horse from being tempted to lay its weight on the bit and use it as a "fifth leg". You can avoid this danger by working with finely tuned halts, driving the horse forwards from behind again and again, and by praising it vocally as soon as the horse relaxes its lower jaw and goes on the bit. It is also a good idea to stop the training session at this stage, as the horse will remember it later and associate the exercise with positive memories.

The Canter

Many horses have difficulties with cantering on a circle in a balanced manner, in particular at the beginning of their schooling. Therefore, the trainer should make sure that the circle is large enough and offers the horse enough space to find its balance.

To begin with, you should leave the lunge reins slack so that the horse is not bothered additionally by the bit in its mouth. At first, only ask for a few strides at the canter and then immediately slow down to the trot or walk. Some horses are afraid of this pace and tend to rush forwards. If the ground is non-slip, you can let it run around a couple of times, but it is better never to let it get to this stage. The canter is one of the last items on the schooling schedule with long reins. Once the horse has reached this level however, it is possible to improve it beautifully, as the trainer has full control over the leg action and can correct any mistakes such as the undesirable dis-united or counter-canter, or the arhythmic engagement of the horse's hindquarters.

The aid for the canter must be applied by means of a distinct half-halt with the lunge reins, which prepares the horse, and then through the voice command. At the same time, swing the lash of the whip in the direction of the stomach and shoulder of the horse so that the horse can position its inner shoulder further forward and you can bring it to strike out at the canter. Never simply use the whip to smack the horse's hindquarters with increasing force until it "falls" into a canter from a fast trot.

Transitions

Apart from voltes and small circles, which we will talk about later, frequent transitions and changes of the tempo in one pace are the best methods to make the horse supple. Always make sure that the exercise is carried out correctly and neatly. Praise the horse for each improvement and don't spend hours trying to solve a particular problem. Instead, choose an exercise at which the horse is proficient, to make the session fun again. Both when changing from a slower pace to a higher one and when slowing down from a faster pace, the power, the thrust, should always come from the hindquarters. With increasing sensitivity of your horse to the aids, the transitions can become more emphatic.

Cantering on long reins is the first step towards collection.

Here you can see clearly how easily you can apply the aids of half-halt and full halt with the inside and outside rein on long reins.

Start off with walk to halt, walk to trot, trot to walk, trot to halt, halt to trot, trot to canter, canter to trot, walk to canter, canter to walk. If the horse is already moving at a collected pace, you can also attempt a halt to canter. If you ask the horse to ride voltes and small circles, the horse needs to have such a degree of collection at the canter that you would have no problem walking alongside it.

Half-Halts and Full Halts

Remember always to ensure that the horse is light on the bit and thus later on the forehand, by using a sensitive advancing hand and the correct timing of half-halts in the mouth. Horses which are given the opportunity to rest their weight on the bit, become insensitive in the mouth and start using it as a "fifth leg". The purpose of the half-halt is to prepare the horse for what is to come, and gain its attention. The full halt should then execute the required task. The half-halt and full halt work together with the action of the horse's hindquarters, which determines the tempo – an increase as well as a reduction of speed. When working a horse from the ground, the trainer has perfect conditions to find the optimum timing for the half-halt, as he can see all four legs of the horse. Any movement towards the inside is prepared by a half-halt when the inner hind leg lifts. As soon as this leg is lifted off the ground, the trainer needs to follow up with a half-halt so that the horse is able to translate the required movement in the period before the foot touches down again.

Lunge Rein around the Hindquarters

Once the horse is working well with long reins and without stress on a circle on both reins, you should proceed to pass the outside lunge rein around the horse's hindquarters at the level of the hocks underneath the tail, rather than over its back.

Warning: when first using this method, many horses react in a panic. Be prepared for it. Initially, you can also get the horse accustomed to the touch of the lunge rein around its hindquarters at the halt, using an assistant to stand at the horse's head. If the horse reacts calmly at the walk, it may well be that the "panic" won't occur until the horse is asked to trot. Respond calmly and in a relaxed manner. This method of attachment of the reins ensures that the

In order to run the lunge rein …

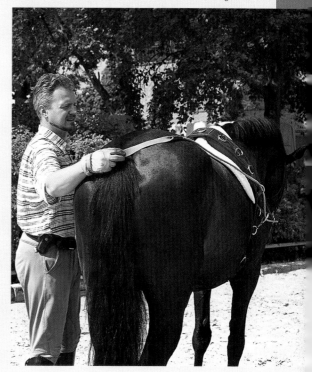

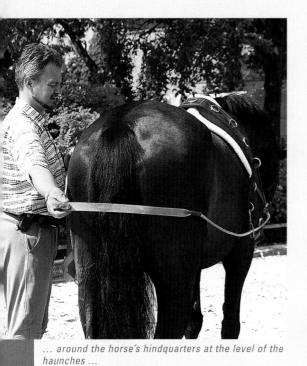

... around the horse's hindquarters at the level of the haunches ...

horse is more securely framed and becomes conscious of the outer side of its body. One of the advantages of long reins is that you have more scope to influence the bend of the horse. The outside lunge rein ensures that the hindquarters cannot swing outward, but instead remain on the circle track.

Important

You need to compensate for the movement of the hindquarters by relaxing the outside lunge rein: otherwise the horse would be jerked in the mouth at every step and the work would be counter-productive. Some horses have an extremely long stride, which leads to a very fidgety handling of the lunge rein. In this case, it is recommended that you pass the outside lunge rein over the horse's back again.

Using the Entire School

Once the horse has learned to perform the exercises so far in the fenced-in lungeing circle well, you can choose to work using the whole school. This gives you far more opportunities to make the horse supple with gymnastics, by changing from straight to bending exercises and back.

Once you leave the circle track and choose the entire school, you will need to walk and run slightly more behind the horse. Beware: some animals then have a tendency to rush off because they feel this position is too forward-driving. If this happens you will need to stay more or less at the shoulder of the horse so that you can regulate the tempo at any time with your voice, half-halts, and the whip.

... the trainer needs to work very gently and slowly.

When the horse has a very long stride, the outside lunge rein (the one around the haunches) needs to give all the time.

The volte is introduced with the inside lunge rein alone. The horse is not pulled inwards.

Voltes

Making the horse perform voltes is another good opportunity to slow the horse down. Introduce the volte with a half-halt. Lead the horse's head slightly inward with the inner lunge rein, walk back a step yourself and increase driving the horse's hindquarters forwards. The inner lunge is repeatedly relaxed in the form of a half-halt to ensure that the horse is not simply pulled to the inside. The outer rein passed around the haunches ensures that the horse stays on the voltes track. The whip points to the shoulder so that the horse does not rush into the centre. The horse is worked outward from the inside, in the same way as under the saddle. In the beginning there will be a bit of confusion, particularly until you have found the correct posture. But then this will become easier and it is a wonderful exercise to control the horse, in particular for the responsiveness and suppleness of the horse. It is best to start the first voltes in the schooling arena in a corner of the school and only later ask the horse to perform these on the long side of the school. The exercise is also an excellent means to work on increasing the tempo and encourage the horse to come onto the bit from the back.

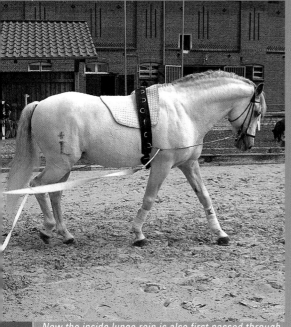

Now the inside lunge rein is also first passed through the D-ring and then attached to the snaffle - in this case with only one deflection roller and set very low down.

The deflection rollers need to be fully opened to be fitted into the rope. It's fiddly work but worth the effort.

Direct Attachment

So far, the type of attachment you've used has prohibited you from performing a smooth change of reins, as you would otherwise have the differently attached lunge reins on the wrong sides.

If everything has gone well up to this point, you (with regard to handling the reins and the whip) and the horse (with regard to becoming accustomed to the reins and the aids) should now be able to apply the direct attachment. For this purpose, the inside lunge rein is also passed from the back to the front first through a ring on the lungeing roller and then hooked into the snaffle ring.

Important

Always use deflection rollers when working the horse in the direct attachment, otherwise the pull on the horse's mouth would be much too severe. Buy rollers of good quality. The more gently the reins work on the horse's mouth, the more sensitive it will be.

At a later stage of the schooling, for horses which have a naturally high head carriage, you should use two deflection rollers per side so that you can move in a comfortable leading position without pulling the horse's head down.

When first starting to use the direct attachment, work the horse in the accustomed lungeing circle until you are sufficient experienced with this attachment.

Horses with a natural high head carriage should always ...

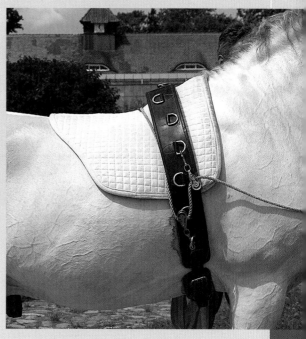

... be attached with two deflection rollers on the outside ...

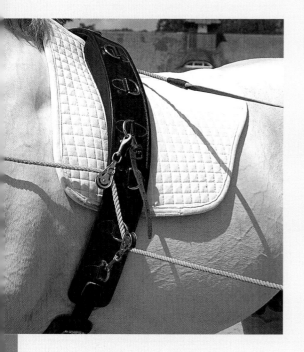

... and on the inside, making sure they are attached level.

Changing the Rein on the Circle

The horse should change reins at least every ten minutes and it needs to be worked on both sides as a matter of course, as it would otherwise be made supple incorrectly. Also, don't work more on the "stiff", tenser side, but make sure that the horse is lunged equally on both sides. Any tension will be released more easily by stretching the muscles rather than pulling the horse together. If the horse has difficulties working on the left rein, the left muscles need to be stretched – in other words, work it on the right rein instead of on the more tense left rein!

Lead the horse towards the centre of the circle as if you were introducing a volte (the inside rein determines the position of the horse's head, the

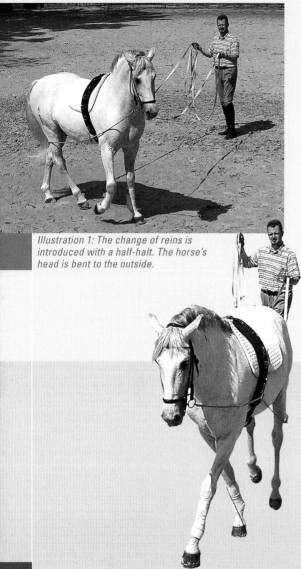

Illustration 1: The change of reins is introduced with a half-halt. The horse's head is bent to the outside.

Illustration 2: The horse is set onto the new rein. The trainer now needs to sort out the lunge reins.

Illustration 3: The trainer then steps behind the horse slightly to one side in order to give the horse sufficient space.

the lunge rein. The horse moves in a small "S" form. Changing the rein this way can often lead to muddled reins, as you need to give with the previously inside rein as soon as it becomes the outside rein. And of course the longer outside rein becomes the shorter inside rein when the change is completed. The more slowly you perform this task, the more experienced you will become in handling the reins.

outside rein keeps the hindquarters "in the frame").

When the horse is at the highest point of the volte, step behind the horse onto the other side of its body and apply driving aids on the other rein.

At the same time, the horse's head needs to be bent into the new inside position with the help of

Important

Make sure when performing figures in the school, and particularly during changes of the rein and voltes, that the horse does not lose its tempo, rhythm and impulsion, otherwise the gymnastic effect will be lost.

Here, you can see very clearly ...

When riding through the corner, the horse is already bent to the inside with its head. Maintain this posture with the help of the lunge reins and lead the horse onto the diagonal. Before you reach the outer track again, change the side you are leading on behind the horse. Working with the two reins in the whole school is the first step to long reining, where you walk close behind the horse and are thus able to apply even more gentle aids, as the lunge reins are shortened back to reins and the horse thus receives the half-halts sooner. However, you need to be absolutely certain that your horse does not kick and that you have completely mastered working with the two reins.

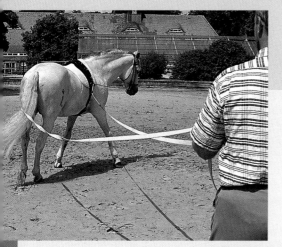

Once the horse has been attached directly, corners are a very good point from which to change the rein.

... how the horse bends to change to the other rein

Changing the Rein Using the Whole School

The easiest change of rein using the entire school is the diagonal change, either through the whole school or to the centre of the long side. This change is performed coming out of a corner, in the same way as it would be done under the saddle.

the horse for changes of the rein, or flexing exercises such as leg-yielding, shoulder-in, and half-pass. If the horse continues to elevate its head and neck on the bit, it is important that you work with two deflection rollers per side to ensure that no incorrect pressure builds up in the horse's mouth and that you yourself can adopt a comfortable posture.

The closer you get behind the horse, the more you also prepare it for carriage driving. However, a shorter whip is more suitable for this kind of work, as for example a long dressage whip or a track and buggy whip.

Working behind the horse leads to a particularly high basic tension and a very direct influence on the horse. However, always make sure that your horse's legs are under control and that it does not lash out. This work forms the preparation for long reining, the real schooling of movement above the ground from the ground.

Working behind the horse serves as a preparation for carriage driving and the schooling of movement above the ground.

Even here, the rein can be placed over the back of the horse ...

... or around the hindquarters to frame the horse better.

Working Behind the Horse

The further you advance with your work with long reins, the closer you will move behind the horse's hindquarters, until eventually you are walking directly behind the horse and only move slightly to the side of

Working With Cavaletti

Working with cavaletti on long reins not only makes for variety in the lesson but can be used particularly for the development and refinement of the rhythm and impulsion of the paces. If you don't have any cavaletti you can use poles on the ground. This work also promotes the boldness and the inner power of the horse: it will become more attentive and will develop greater self-confidence.

Note

■ ■ ■ ■

Instead of using poles on the ground for this work, it is better to use square-section four-by-fours. Poles lying loosely on the ground can roll away when the horse knocks them during work, and then roll between its legs.

The distances between the poles should be around 80 to 90 centimetres at the walk, 120 to 130 centimetres at the trot, and around 300 centimetres at the canter. Of course, the distance is dependent on the size of the horse and the length of its stride. Let your horse walk over the poles and then place the poles at such a distance that it will have to stretch itself a bit further in order to keep the distance. In this manner you achieve an effect which strengthens the gymnastic ability of the horse. Please take care at the canter: some horses get too excited at this pace, so that any gymnastic effect would be lost. If this happens, don't perform the exercise at the canter.

School Track Figures

Let your imagination run free when working with long reins. Anything that the horse enjoys and which does not force it into having to face impossible problems is permitted.

If the circle is large enough, the trainer can also work in wonderful figures of eight. The final effect is a combination of changing the rein through the circle and voltes. The important thing is that you prepare the horse in good time with half-halts and get it into position, without pulling it around with

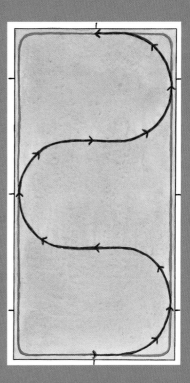

Serpentines using the whole arena are also very well suited for work with long reins.

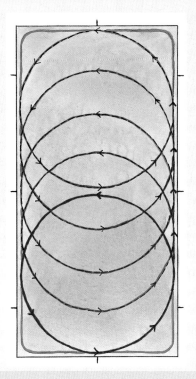

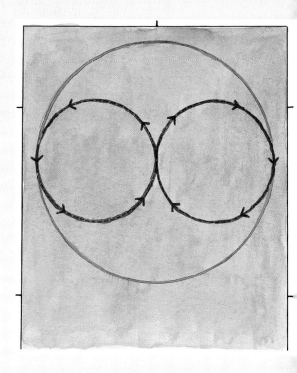

The wandering circle through the length of the school trains the horse's balance and responsiveness to the aids.

Changes of the rein in S-form can also be performed within the circle.

the inside rein. And make sure you take note of the position of your body.

If you have an entire school, another exercise, the wandering circle, can also be carried out. Start quite normally on the circle track and then lead your horse further into the middle of the arena with each circle, away from the fence.

This teaches the horse to detach itself from the boundary of the fence and to concentrate more on your aids. You can lead the wandering circle down the entire length of the school.

If your arena is large enough, you can also combine a few low fences. You just need to have enough space that you don't have to jump with your horse during each circle. Some experts build a jump on both long sides of the school and then lead the horse over the fences in ever-varying

combinations by making it perform changes of the reins and voltes. However, care is needed.

The larger you keep the school figures, the more mobile and fit you yourself have to be if it should become necessary, for example, to jump a larger fence at higher speed. And in all these exercises you need to maintain a light contact with the horse and not let yourself be pulled around.

Main Faults

When working with horses, the greatest mistake is and always will be going too fast. Instead of working long enough on the correct execution and translation of less difficult exercises until these have really sunk in, many riders and lungeing peopleover-ambitiuosly move on too fast.

The horse is too slow or too fast:

Always take note of your own body language. Are you standing in the correct position in relation to the horse, are you slowing it down, or are you driving it forwards too much? Let friends, or even better an experienced teacher, correct your mistakes. Check with a horse that is too slow whether you are hauling too much on the lunge reins. Or did you forget the forward-driving whip? Are you standing too far away from the shoulder of the horse and thereby slowing it down unintentionally? If the horse is too fast, are you continuously driving it forwards from behind with the whip as a reflex action? Or are you standing too far behind the horse, so that you emanate a forward-driving force? Has your horse really understood what you want? Is it physically and mentally mature enough to execute the tasks required of it?

The horse does not try to go on the bit,
does not stretch forwards and downward:

Have a vet check whether the horse's legs and back are injured in any way, or whether there is an underlying tension somewhere; a pinched nerve or anything similar. The same goes for the teeth. Many horses are simply in pain due to the bit. Allow the horse enough time to stretch. Do not drive it forward too much or too little. Maintain soft hands, offering the horse scope to stretch downward. Keep contact with its mouth, drive it forward from behind and give gently with the reins, even if the horse initially does not stretch downward. Be patient!

The horse does not come to a halt:

Work in a fenced-off area. Position it distinctly with its head bent outward and use the half-halts more than distinctly once or twice.

The horse breaks away when worked in an unfenced school or arena:

Go back to your last stage of schooling in the fenced-off circle and check your own pecking order in relation to the horse. Then start by changing to the open arena, by staying close to the horse and not allowing it too much freedom of the reins. And avoid those school figures which do not require the horse to be on the bit. When, and only when, you are sure that you have the horse under control, move away from the fencing. Concentrate fully on the horse. The earlier you learn to recognise even the slightest attempt at ill-humour and signs of rebellion, the faster you will be able to react. Check whether you are asking too much or too little of your horse.

The horse drops over the inner shoulder

In this case, your influence with the inner lunge rein is too severe, while the contact with the outside rein is inadequate. The horse is merely being pulled around. Under certain circumstances, the circle may be too small for the horse, so that it cannot find its balance.

Working with long reins is the precursor to the school above the ground and thereby to the highest art of equitation.

Looking Ahead

Working with long reins can be the start of a long and fruitful process of training from the ground, even for those movements only required in the classic art of movements above the ground. It offers the horse the opportunity to achieve something wonderful without the weight of the rider. Even old horses can be made suppler with this work. And older horsemen and women can also perform good work with long reins, long after they start to experience problems in the saddle.

When you have taken the effort to perform lungeing and long reining, not as an easy alternative to exercising the horse, but in recognition of the beneficial gymnastic and schooling effect, you will find that you are equipped with a means to cure almost all problems which might occur during your career as a rider. And it is definitely worth the effort, instead of just going to equitation seminars, to ask an expert and able person to teach you about working from the ground. A healthy, energetic and mentally well-balanced horse will be grateful to you for many years.